CalmUp®
JOURNEY

T0099819

CALMUP® Journey

Also by Lorie S. Gose, Psy.D.

CalmUp® Journey Pages: Your Keepsafe for Better Days
Published by Balboa Press

CalmUp®
JOURNEY

Your Daily Ascending Tool for Better Days

Lorie S. Gose, Psy.D.

Foreword by Rabbi Benjamin Arnold

BALBOA.
PRESS
A DIVISION OF HAY HOUSE

Copyright © 2011 Lorie S. Gose, Psy.D.

All rights reserved. No part of this book may be used or reproduced by any means, graphic, electronic, or mechanical, including photocopying, recording, taping or by any information storage retrieval system without the written permission of the publisher except in the case of brief quotations embodied in critical articles and reviews.

Balboa Press books may be ordered through booksellers or by contacting:

Balboa Press
A Division of Hay House
1663 Liberty Drive
Bloomington, IN 47403
www.balboapress.com
1 (877) 407-4847

Because of the dynamic nature of the Internet, any web addresses or links contained in this book may have changed since publication and may no longer be valid. The views expressed in this work are solely those of the author and do not necessarily reflect the views of the publisher, and the publisher hereby disclaims any responsibility for them.

The author of this book does not dispense medical advice or prescribe the use of any technique as a form of treatment for physical, emotional, or medical problems without the advice of a physician, either directly or indirectly. The intent of the author is only to offer information of a general nature to help you in your quest for emotional and spiritual well-being. In the event you use any of the information in this book for yourself, which is your constitutional right, the author and the publisher assume no responsibility for your actions.

Copy Editing: Marj Hahne
Logo Design: Debbie Oberhausen
Cover Design: Andrew Mays
Book Design: Katie Schneider
Author Photograph: Stephanie Block

Certain stock imagery © Thinkstock.
Any people depicted in stock imagery provided by Thinkstock are models,
and such images are being used for illustrative purposes only.

ISBN: 978-1-4525-3445-9 (e)
ISBN: 978-1-4525-3444-2 (sc)

Library of Congress Control Number: 2011906325

Printed in the United States of America

Balboa Press rev. date: 10/4/2011

for David, my husband and life partner—
for our journey together

Look at this day,
For it is life,
The very life of life.
In its brief course lie all
The realities and verities of existence,
The bliss of growth,
The splendor of action,
The glory of power—

For yesterday is but a dream,
And tomorrow is only a vision.
But today, well lived,
Makes every yesterday a dream of happiness
And every tomorrow a vision of hope.

Look well, therefore, to this day.

—Sanskrit Proverb

Contents

Foreword

*T*his morning the chimney sweep guy called. Apparently, it's been over two years since we've had him out to the house, and, according to our local fire marshal's standards, we're overdue for a good cleaning. Yes, it's time to update the home-improvement plan! The ladder is ready and waiting, but where shall I start? Perhaps with the following question: *How can I …?* How can I make my home safer, more comforting, more colorful, beautiful, energy-efficient, nurturing, peaceful, joyful, meaningful, and welcoming for myself, my family, and our guests? Okay. That's a start, but then what?

The book before you is like a homeowner's manual shared by a seasoned and skilled home inspector. It's a *life-liver's* manual, offering a carefully honed, step-by-step method for improving life, individually and collectively, within and beyond your home. It inspires and guides a journey of *life* improvement with a ladder of its own, one well worth ascending (and descending) on a daily basis.

CalmUp® Journey: Your Daily Ascending Tool for Better Days is different from other self-help books. Though compact, it considers the whole. Dr. Gose encourages and guides us to make a conscious account of the whole of our human experience—intrapersonal and interpersonal. As promised, she invites us to integrate biology, psychology, sociology, and spirituality as we create and implement a vision of what can be.

And the spirituality she offers is refreshing in its ability to get to *the heart of the matter*, in every sense of that phrase. Rather than be seduced by the easy roads of "feel good" spirituality, she shares a definition of spirituality searching for balance through the disciplined practice of giving. It is rooted in the tradition of service to others—a tradition beating at the heart of all spiritual and religious paths. Here we're offered a path, not just to *feeling* better, but to *being* better, becoming better people. *CalmUp®️ Journey* is an echo of an ancient calling (accompanied by a contemporary curriculum) to improve the character of humanity, not just our own personal experience.

CalmUp®️ Journey empowers us to transcend the limitations of conventional self-help methods, moving us from mere personal empowerment to transcendence and transformation. As such, it is an honor and a privilege for me to endorse Dr. Gose's invitation to join her, as she draws upon her wealth of personal and professional experience, research and study, in adding "ever-expanding insight and awareness [and joy and peace] into what it means to be a whole human being."

As you set forth on this journey, allow me to invoke another one via my translation of Genesis 28: 10-17 from the Hebrew:

> And Jacob journeyed forth from the Well-of-Seven, and went towards Eight-Fold Bliss. And suddenly, he came upon a place and set up to spend the night there. As the sun came down to set, he took stones from that place, setting his head upon them, and he slept in the place. And he dreamt. There! A ladder, upright, reaching towards the earth, with its top stretching to the heavens. And there! Angels, Divine Beings, messengers, ascending and descending with it…

> "There, now. I am with you, a guardian guiding your way, and I will not leave you until all that has been promised has been fulfilled." And Jacob started from his sleep, and said, "Ah, yes. Holy-bliss is in this place, and I, well, I did not know it. And he was overcome with wonder and awe, and a good dose of fear, and said, "How…how wondrous is this place. It can be! It can be none other than a Divine sanctuary, a gateway to the heavens."

Among the "stones" on the pages that follow are gems. Collect them. Write about them in your journal. Sleep on them. And when the sun rises again, I pray with confidence that you, too, will find yourself overflowing with gratitude and wonder at having found yourself in *this* place, inspired by *this* vision, equipped with *this* ladder, and accompanied by angels like Lorie, as we jointly lift ourselves and our world, one rung at a time, closer to an all-embracing bliss.

We can exist in a house, or we can *live* in a sanctuary. Now is the time to update that home-improvement plan, to call the chimney sweep, break out the ladder, and begin the ascent, again.

May the journey be blessed!

Rabbi Benjamin Arnold

Preface

The health of humanity—a highfalutin phrase, I know, but the best to capture my deepest commitment. My life experiences, education, and career have brought me right to this place—one of ever-expanding insight and awareness into what it means to be a whole human being. I have been both captivated and intrigued by the integration of our physiology, thought processes, emotions, behaviors, environmental influences, and spirit. The CalmUp® Journey, the culmination of my work to date, is a one-page (two-sided), self-guided form designed to create better days by leading you to your own insights and answers—around a troubling issue, an objective, an existential inquiry, a practical or moral dilemma, a musing—along your journey of personal growth and understanding.

I've wanted to be a psychologist since I was seven. That or a prima ballerina, but when my family moved from San Diego, California, to a kibbutz in Israel, my ballet lessons went the way of Baskin-Robbins and my phonograph. At the kibbutz, even though I lived in the children's house, where all the kids slept and gathered according to age, I spent more time with my parents than I ever had before. One day, just wanting to hang out with my mom while she knit or wrote to family in the States, I searched the bookshelf for something to read in English and became enthralled by the little boy's face on the cover of one of her paperbacks. I read *Dibs: In Search of Self*,[1] written by a clinical psychologist, over and over, to understand how Dr. Axline helped Dibs. I knew that someday I, too, would support others to have better days.

---

1   Virginia M. Axline, *Dibs: In Search of Self* (New York: Ballantine Books, 1964).

When I began my studies in psychology ten years later, I steered away from working with children, believing at the time that working all day with children in need would compromise my availability for my own, future child. I chose instead to specialize in health psychology, with the aim to work in infertility. I focused my early graduate studies on the "biopsychosocial model,"[2] an approach designed to encompass all health and disease. This model proposes that, in order to assess a person's health status, we need to consider the interaction of the biological, psychological, and social factors. Such global, rather than isolated, assessment allows for more comprehensive and effective treatment.

Only after the completion of my graduate training did I notice issues of a spiritual nature being raised by my psychotherapy patients. (The medical model taught us to consider people coming for psychotherapy as patients, not clients.) I wondered if patients during my training *had* brought up spiritual issues but I hadn't paid any attention because that realm fell outside the model. As I became increasingly aware of the significance and prevalence of the spiritual dimension, I incorporated spiritual ideas into the psychological component of the biopsychosocial model.

As a new psychologist in 1993, I continued to develop my personal style of cognitive-behavioral psychotherapy. My allowing for a spiritual component seemed to magnetize to my office more and more patients with spiritual issues. I came to privately think of myself as a closet cognitive-behavioral-spiritual psychologist. Over time, and with thanks to my patients' genuineness, my comfort level in addressing the spiritual expanded. I discovered that this holistic approach—one that considers the spiritual as well as the biological, psychological, and social—significantly decreased the length of treatment needed. I now naturally integrate spiritual beliefs, as do many psychotherapists, according to what's personally meaningful to the individual patient.

While explaining my psychotherapeutic method during new-patient consultations, I found myself drawing a circle divided into four equal sections instead of a three-

---

2   Gary E. Schwartz, "Testing the Biopsychosocial Model: The Ultimate Challenge Facing Behavioral Medicine?" *Journal of Consulting and Clinical Psychology* 50, no. 6 (1982): 1040–1053.

sided triangle. The CalmUp® Journey germinated from the user-friendly language I used to explain to my patients the bio, psycho, social, *and* spiritual components of this model. How my four-part circle became a seven-tier "ladder" owes first to the vision of my mother, Nirmal Almeida, who, after reviewing my paradigm, dreamt about a rainbow model, with its seven colors. After listening to three of my audio mentors, Dr. Caroline Myss,[3] Dr. Anodea Judith,[4] and Dr. Rick Jarrow,[5] I considered how the four-part, biopsychosocial-spiritual model might fit with the seven-tier, human energy system. Thus was born the CalmUp® Journey in its current form, with a base "START" level, a top "FINISH" level, and five intermediary levels. The five intermediary levels correspond to the chapter titles with the following headings: Birth, Live, Inward, Society, and Spirit.

Although this tool has found its way to you and me, I initially developed it to support my patients in my private practice as a psychologist. My goal had been to provide high-quality, solution-focused treatment over a short duration (often no more than ten sessions) and to teach patients how to empower themselves rather than become dependent on me, the clinician.

At one point in my practice, when it seemed like most everyone was in the process of terminating treatment, I was hired to work in reproductive medicine. I first sought that position ten years earlier and, hoping to fulfill my career goals, had remained in touch with the company. For reasons pertaining to intellectual property rights, I chose to not teach the CalmUp® Journey during my five-year employment. Instead, I began personally experimenting with the tool when my life became the definition of chaos, with perimenopause to boot. A higher source seemed to orchestrate one new challenge after another that coincided with the ordered levels of the tool. I was able to refine the tool's functionality, level by level, while refining my own life! With regular

---

3   Caroline Myss, *Energy Anatomy: The Science of Personal Power, Spirituality, and Health* (Boulder, CO: Sounds True, 1996), 6 audio cassettes.

4   Anodea Judith, *The Chakra System: A Complete Course in Self-Diagnosis and Healing* (Boulder, CO: Sounds True, 2000), 6 audio cassettes.

5   Rick Jarrow, *Your Life's Work: The Ultimate Anti-Career Guide* (Boulder, CO: Sounds True, 1998), 6 audio cassettes.

use of the tool, I felt better physically, became highly skilled in my position, saved my marriage, became a better mother, and improved my other relationships. Overall, I became a happier person. My closest friends, with whom I had shared the tool, also reported benefits in their lives.

I have since changed my career goals and have been able to share the tool with others seeking better days. Presently, I enjoy working part-time at two nursing facilities, where I regularly support residents with such issues as adjusting to long-term care, coping with traumatic brain injury, and living with numerous medical challenges. Because most of the residents with whom I work are physically unable to write, they complete the CalmUp® Journey through verbal self-expression.

A lineage of scholars conducted the classic research on cognitive and behavioral models of psychotherapy, but it was the work and writing of Dr. David D. Burns[6] that set the groundwork for me as a clinician. And Dr. Paul Block, my graduate school mentor, encouraged me to explore what is personally meaningful and modeled creativity to that end.

During a two-year period, I proposed a scientific research study of the CalmUp® Journey to both undergraduate and graduate psychology departments. Although the project didn't come to fruition, if you would like to participate in a less scientific—though still valuable—research project, your completion of the questionnaire at the end of the book (see Appendix C) is greatly appreciated.

The personal choices we make—essential for our own well-being—have an impact on others, too. My intention is that the CalmUp® Journey will foster our joyful and peaceful existence, individually and collectively.

---

6   David D. Burns, *Feeling Good: The New Mood Therapy* (New York: Signet, 1980).

Acknowledgments

Cultivating this book, *CalmUp® Journey: Your Daily Ascending Tool for Better Days*, to fruition could not have been possible without the help of numerous people, to whom I'm indebted. The term "audio mentors" best describes the many authors and speakers I've listened to on tape and CD while commuting behind the wheel. To mention all of them, I would've needed to keep a log for the past twenty years. This body of remarkable teachers includes Louise Hay, Zig Ziglar, Neale Donald Walsch, Caroline Myss, Joan Borysenko, Deepak Chopra, Wayne Dyer, Cheryl Richardson, Shakti Gawain, Eckhart Tolle, David Reynolds, Naomi Rosenblatt, Anodea Judith, Sharon Franquemont, Gary Zukav, and His Holiness the Dalai Lama.

A few authors, Lionel Fisher, Sarah Susanka, and Julie Ziglar Norman, have mentored me by answering questions, sharing their experiences, and helping me explore ideas. Dr. Philip Incao introduced me to several works by Rudolf Steiner and modeled what it means to be selfless. I also give honorable mention to Micah and Desiree Springer, at Vital Yoga, along with their staff of teachers, who've supported the safe opening of my heart. I give my gratitude to Dr. Susan Messina, Ula Heroux, Mary Ray, Alison Stallcup, Elizabeth Muxi, and other friends and colleagues who've reviewed the development of my work over the years.

I'm most lovingly grateful to my husband, David, who patiently supported me while I experienced my own challenging movement along the CalmUp® Journey so that I could share it with full confidence and integrity. His love is truly blissful.

Among my most important teachers of unconditional love are my parents. I thank my mother, Nirmal Almeida, and my stepfather, Avi Almeida, who were instrumental in the early editing process and faithfully supportive of my decision making. Thank you to my father, Bernard Resnick, who served as my coach in 2009, helping me stay on track and listening to my occasional venting. His companion, Chris Schoonhoven, has remained a wellspring of encouragement.

Elders in my life, both living and passed, continue to inspire me. My parents-in-law, Wade and Laverne Gose, would've been among my greatest supporters were they alive today. I gain strength from my living relatives and my ancestors who've set the stage for my life today. My sister, Robin Resnick, inspires genuineness. Children have also been powerful for my own path of ascending—specifically, my son, Aaron, a bright light in my life. I'm humbled daily as he guides me to parent with compassion. I'm additionally grateful to my professors, patients, residents, students, colleagues, employers, and friends who have shared and modeled their wisdom.

Thank you to my gifted current editor, Marj Hahne, as well as my previous editor, Debra Miess. Their creativity and understanding of my ideas and objectives supported the emergence of this work with beautiful language. I give praise to my graphic artist, Debbie Oberhausen, who created the beautiful CalmUp® logo. Thank you also to the staff at Balboa Press, who earnestly helped this work materialize. I will continue to share this work with appreciation to my Denver SBDC business counselors, Jayne Reiter and Chuck Hahn.

I'm especially grateful to you, the reader, for joining me in creating better days. Thank you for allowing me the opportunity to ascend with you.

With appreciation,

Lorie S. Gose, Psy.D.
Lakewood, Colorado
January 11, 2011

Introduction

The sound of your alarm clock bolts you awake like an ambush. You should've gone to bed earlier, you tell yourself, but you didn't want the weekend to end, so you stayed up late. Your body aches; your eyelids are impossibly heavy. If only you had just one more day off to get done some of the things on your to-do list. Now you have to get up and go to work. You don't even like your job, but you go there day in and day out. "You're lucky to have a job," everyone tells you. You've been doing the best you can, taking care of your responsibilities, but you wish your life could be different, easier. Argh. You hit the snooze button.

You awaken to your favorite music on your iPod. You're feeling good after a quiet evening of reading and a full night's sleep. You spring out of bed, make a cup of tea or coffee, and move to your favorite sitting area. You'd set the alarm thirty minutes early, so you're feeling the spaciousness of the morning. You wrap yourself in a soft afghan and light a candle. You pull out a blank CalmUp® Journey, then close your eyes and quiet your mind. You ask from your heart a "How can I..." question about a troubling issue or personal situation. Moving from the bottom to the top of the page, you respond to each question, remaining gentle with yourself. You make a conscious choice that will forward the day. You trust that you're right where you need to be.

Which Monday morning would you prefer? Do you feel you have a choice in the way your mornings play out? What about the rest of your day? And the rest of your life?

These two scenarios don't represent good and bad, right and wrong. They're just choices we make. Perhaps you relate to parts of each; perhaps neither scenario describes your current or desired typical morning. Still, do you feel overwhelmed at times, uncertain about your life path, longing for a better day? Do you know you need to make a change, but the thought of doing something new is daunting? Hey, many of us are not really sure of what we need or where we're going. All of us could use a hand.

Enter the CalmUp® Journey.

The CalmUp® Journey isn't a magical formula for happiness. The truth is, you don't have to *do* anything, let alone complete a form, to experience peace and joy. It's too easy, however, to let the pace and distractions of contemporary life misguide us about what we want and derail our best intentions. What the CalmUp® Journey facilitates, then, is your intentionality, your choosing with full awareness; and the regular practice of completing the tool can revitalize that awareness so that you're operating at your height of power daily.

Of course, you don't always feel overwhelmed. Sometimes you know precisely where you've been and where you're headed. You're filled with feelings of appreciation and abundance. Can your day really get any better?

Yes. There's no limit to the quality of your day. The paradox, however, is that improving your own day involves serving others. In other words, true self-help is really about "other-help." The CalmUp® Journey's help is multifold: you'll learn a new tool to support you in improving your day and, in turn, the day of those around you.

The name, CalmUp® Journey, is derived from the structure of the one-page (two-sided), self-guided form (see next page and also Appendix B). You'll begin with a "How can I..." question and investigate your relationship with that issue through multiple lenses, moving *up* the page. So, referring to the form, you'll begin at "Start" in the bottom left-hand box and end at "Finish" in the top left-hand box. For each CalmUp® Journey you take, you'll ascend through the seven levels (I–VII) by completing the form from the bottom row to the top row and from the left column to the right column.

CalmUp® Journey

Date: _____

Instructions: Begin in the bottom row. Enter your responses, moving up from left to right.

Deep healing breath; conscious choices **FINISH →** *(1) Today I choose to empower myself by* *(2) I share/serve by*	 _____ Peace & joy rating 1–10 (low to high)
Spirit	**Spirit**
Illusions (First clear your mind on the back of this page.) *I believed*	Creative openings *I open to*
Society	**Society**
Poor choices impacting others *My poor choices have included*	Being of service *With integrity, I will*
Inward	**Inward**
Disheartening image *I have pictured myself*	Self-loving visualization *Today I visualize myself*
Live	**Live**
Disturbing physical symptoms *I have experienced*	Positive affirmation for your health *I am*
Birth	**Birth**
Painful emotions *I have felt*	Peaceful emotions *As my authentic self, I feel*
One issue **START →** *How can I*	 _____ Peace & joy rating 1–10 (low to high)

*Can you conceive that your responses in the left column are not "bad" and those in the right column are not "good"? We need **all** parts of ourselves to create our wholeness.*

Copyright © 2011 by Lorie S. Gose, Psy.D. All Rights Reserved.

www.drloriegose.com

Clear your mind by listing or journaling all your <u>worries, fears, and discouraging thoughts</u> about your question.

Allow your mind to become radiant by <u>brainstorming encouraging and hopeful ideas</u> about your question. What statements might a best friend, lover, or counselor offer?

Copyright © 2011 by Lorie S. Gose, Psy.D. All Rights Reserved.
www.drloriegose.com

A sample completed version of the CalmUp® Journey is provided (Appendix A) so that you can get a better feel for how the tool works. Other sample responses are given throughout the book.

This Daily Ascending Tool can help illuminate and untangle the unprocessed emotions and inhibiting beliefs that tie up the energy you could otherwise direct toward supporting yourself and others. By the time you get to the top of the CalmUp® Journey, you may have a new outlook on your question and greater access to your authentic self—even after the first ascent.

As you become more genuine with yourself, you'll likely find that you become more connected with others around you. No matter what situation you find yourself in, you can be stronger and, at the same time, gentler—the same composition of "tough love." You may find that you have more energy to *want* to help others; feeling like you *should* help others will only deplete you and diminish both giver and receiver. Along the CalmUp® Journey, you reclaim your essential self and determine how to be empowered today.

The CalmUp® Journey is neutral, yet depends on your honesty. Your thoughts and feelings are all valid—not right or wrong, okay or not okay. You'll soon discover that there are many ways to complete your Daily Ascending Tool.

If your mornings are full, you could complete the tool before bed and then do a brief review before heading out the door. I prefer to start my CalmUp® Journey before bed, completing the bottom five levels, then completing the top two levels the next morning. On the days I don't feel like writing or journaling, I'll answer the questions silently to myself while walking my dogs in the morning. You may think more clearly in a quiet, comfortable space, or on the bus or train ride to work. You may wish to ritualize this personal time by writing with a special pen or lighting a candle. Developing a routine that works best for you will help ensure you stick with it.

How will you complete the CalmUp® Journey? Can you dedicate time for yourself—twenty to thirty minutes in the morning after waking or in the evening before bed—to set up your intention for the day ahead? If you're very busy or have a challenging question, you may want to take more contemplative time for each of the seven levels. For instance, you could dedicate a week to work through a question by focusing on one level each day for seven consecutive mornings. This would allow you ample time to process your concern and provide a new perspective for the coming week.

Are you concerned about not having time to fit one more task into your life? As you create intimate time to explore your concerns and curiosities, you'll begin to think, feel, and act differently. You'll become a priority in your life, and you'll naturally restructure your time to support only your authentic commitments. Although the CalmUp® Journey is designed to be used as a daily tool, you're encouraged to skip one day per week, perhaps Saturday or Sunday, to take a breather from all that change!

Funny how a voyage can feel intimidating and longer the first time you take it. Each time you complete the CalmUp® Journey, it will become more familiar—and feel less time-consuming. Your first CalmUp® Journey may take an hour to complete; with practice, you can expect to complete a CalmUp® Journey in twenty to thirty minutes.

At the beginning of any new adventure, staying on course can be challenging. To support your ascent, the CalmUp® Journey Sample Version (Appendix A) provides full prompts and sample responses, and gives markers—underlined phrases that serve as mapping points to help keep you on track. For instance, disturbing physical symptoms appears in the left-hand box of Level III, while positive affirmation for your health appears in the right-hand box. With time and practice, you'll be able to complete the guide simply by following these reminder phrases, isolated on the Do-It-Yourself Version (Appendix B).

As you step onto this path, can you stay open, can you stay the course, if you notice yourself reacting to and making judgments about the language on the tool and in the book? For instance, depending on your stance toward spirituality and religion, the Level VI heading, "Spirit," may make you want to stop before you even start. Language has the ability both to connect and to offend. Can you allow yourself to just observe what arises for you, trust the intention behind the tool, and discover how to make the CalmUp® Journey meaningful to you?

Every day, as you use the CalmUp® Journey, remind yourself that you build your personal power by gently monitoring your beliefs, thoughts, behaviors, and choices rather than by trying to control those of others.

Are you ready to begin your CalmUp® Journey?

Key Points for Introduction

✓ For each CalmUp® Journey, you'll ascend through the seven levels by completing the tool from the bottom row to the top row and from the left column to the right column.

✓ Underlined words are map coordinates to help keep you on track.

✓ There are many ways to complete your Daily Ascending Tool. Develop a routine that works best for you.

✓ Although the CalmUp® Journey is designed to be used as a daily tool, you're encouraged to skip one day per week, perhaps Saturday or Sunday, to take a breather from all that change!

CALMUP® Journey

Chapter 1

Level I:
Are You Ready to Change, Heal, and Live Fully?

Mental health is a function of choice.
The more choices we are able to exercise,
the happier we are likely to be.

Gordon Livingston, M.D.
Too Soon Old, Too Late Smart: Thirty Things You Need to Know Now

Ask the Question

We all want to change, to grow, to move forward. Sometimes we want a big change, like a new place of residence, an expanded family, a different career, or a new partner. Other times, we want a small change, like a clean kitchen, deeper connection with a friend, or a project completed. Still other times, we just want more money to buy things: a new wardrobe, car, or computer. Ultimately, we want to feel good. And, despite all the psychological and spiritual literature about inner well-being, we tend to believe we'll feel better *when*: when we have a new job, an organized closet, a regular Friday night date—when our life is somehow different on the outside.

Do you want to have a better day *today*?

The CalmUp® Journey is a daily journey. And it begins with a question—an open-ended one: *How can I...?* The beauty of an open-ended question is that it expands the field of possibility, allowing answers to emerge from outside your inhibiting beliefs and self-concept. This requires letting go of judgments about where you are now and trusting that there *is* an answer, even if it's only the answer for today.

Your questions may repeat or vary from day to day. Use the CalmUp® Journey for guidance—and ascent!—during life's challenges, transitions, and crises, and especially to enhance daily life experiences.

If you're unsure about the kinds of questions to ask, consider these:

Sample Questions:

Personal:

> » *How can I stop feeling stuck in my life?*
> » *How can I start feeling fulfilled today?*
> » *How can I clean up the piles next to my bed today?*
> » *How can I let go of items in my life that I don't need?*
> » *How can I combine my self-comforting needs with my nutritional needs?*
> » *How can I cope with having to live in this place?*
> » *How can I become a more loving person?*

Relationship:

> » *How can I communicate genuinely with [name]?*
> » *How can I develop a healthy intimate relationship?*
> » *How can I get any sleep when [name] turns on the light in the middle of the night?*
> » *How can I adjust to living with [name]?*
> » *How can I forgive [name]?*
> » *How can I ever get over the divorce?*
> » *How can I show [name] how much he/she means to me?*

Family:

> *How can I spend quality time with my family today?*
> *How can I take time for myself when I would be taking time away from my family?*
> *How can I show my family that I love them?*
> *How can I behave like a mature person with my parents?*
> *How can I guide my children without too much discipline?*
> *How can I get my family to clean up after themselves?*
> *How can I tell my cousin that I can't afford to fly to his wedding?*

Work:

> *How can I find a meaningful job?*
> *How can I continue in this job when it's completely unfulfilling?*
> *How can I balance my work life and my home life?*
> *How can I make it to work on time?*
> *How can I leave work at work and not bring it home?*
> *How can I ask my boss for a raise?*
> *How can I motivate my team to work harder and more efficiently?*

Finances:

> *How can I pay my bills?*
> *How can I get out from under my debt?*
> *How can I stop spending so much money on [shoes, cigarettes, etc.]?*
> *How can I pay for my kids' college education when I haven't saved enough for my retirement?*
> *How can I make time to work on our household finances?*
> *How can I get my personal finances in order?*
> *How can I start managing my spending?*

Health:

» *How can I continue to live with this pain?*

» *How can I survive the effects of chemotherapy?*

» *How can I start exercising even 15 minutes a day?*

» *How can I stop eating so much junk food?*

» *How can I lose 10 pounds?*

» *How can I get at least 8 hours of sleep every night?*

» *How can I get myself to an A.A. meeting today?*

Faith:

» *How can I trust that I'm right where I need to be?*

» *How can I let go of my worries and surrender to a higher power?*

» *How can I have faith that everything will turn out all right?*

» *How can I even think about going back to church after all these years?*

» *How can I trust in a God that would allow this to happen?*

» *How can I begin to relate to God as my friend?*

» *How can I remember to think about God's grace in the middle of my day?*

Daily Life Experiences:

» *How can I have some fun today?*

» *How can I live my "best life" today?*

» *How can I feel happy today?*

» *How can I create the kind of day I will always remember?*

» *How can I start living today without the fear of the past?*

» *How can I integrate meditation into my day?*

» *How can I schedule time to make love today?*

One key to a purposeful ascent is to <u>write your question in line with your values</u>. Consider which of the following questions per pair fits your personal values:

How can I earn a million dollars?
OR
How can I support others to get what they want and know in my heart that what I'm doing is for the highest good?

How can I feel like I'm part of my community?
OR
How can I give my time and contribute to my community?

How can I get the promotion I deserve?
OR
How can I continue to do the highest-quality work with integrity and be compensated accordingly?

Your Turn:

Although you're just getting started on your CalmUp® Journey, can you consider that Level I is exactly where you need to *be* right now? And can you imagine that you actually don't have to *do* anything to be empowered today?

Remember what all your teachers said about there being no such thing as a stupid question? What's weighing on your mind? What's your most pressing question today? What heartache, distress, quandary, or curiosity needs some movement? Take a moment to be still, perhaps closing your eyes. When you're ready, complete this box, the bottom one in the left column, on the CalmUp® Journey (Appendix B):

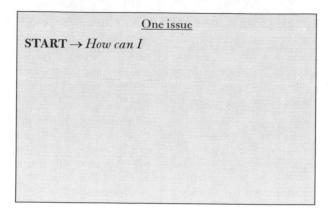

Rate Your Experience

Because the CalmUp® Journey is about creating enduring positive change, you'll need a reference point, a baseline, against which to evaluate your progress. After writing your question, you'll rate, on a 1-to-10 scale, how much peace and joy you're experiencing in relation to your question. A rating of 1 indicates the lowest degree of peace and joy; a rating of 10, the highest.

To better understand the Level I process, see these sample pairings of questions and base ratings:

Sample Ratings:

<table>
<tr>
<td>One issue
START → *How can I **get past the pain of John's death?***</td>
<td>

1
——————
Rating 1–10</td>
</tr>
</table>

<table>
<tr>
<td>One issue
START → *How can I **continue to work for a company whose values I don't respect?***</td>
<td>

3
——————
Rating 1–10</td>
</tr>
</table>

One issue	
START → *How can I fully engage in this beautiful day before me?*	**9** Rating 1–10

One issue	
START → *How can I lose weight when my foot hurts and I can't exercise?*	**2** Rating 1–10

One issue	
START → *How can I make fun a priority today before I go back to work tomorrow?*	**7** Rating 1–10

Your Turn:

Notice how much peace and joy you're presently experiencing in relation to your question. Move horizontally to the bottom box in the right column of the form, and rate your experience without judging it.

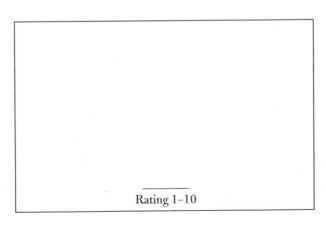

Rating 1–10

Follow Your Own Direction

When you choose a "How can I..." question, your inclination may be to (1) try to change someone else, (2) do something helpful for someone else at your own expense, or (3) do something hurtful to someone else. If these or other unconstructive questions arise, sink deeper into your essential self. When you follow your authentic direction with the CalmUp® Journey, you (1) focus on changing only yourself, (2) do acts of kindness in the best interests of all parties, and (3) come from a place of love.

Key Points for Level I

✓ Ask a "How can I..." question for the day and assign a baseline rating, from 1 (lowest) to 10 (highest).

✓ Being at your height of power means consciously choosing your attitude for the day and what's meaningful for you and your life.

✓ One key to a purposeful ascent is to write your question in line with your values.

✓ You don't have to *do* anything to feel better in any moment.

CalmUp® Journey

Chapter 2

Level II:
What Are You Prepared to Birth Today?

Truth is that which does not contaminate you, but empowers you.

Gary Zukav
The Seat of the Soul

Remember Your Core

The CalmUp® Journey appears to be composed of two columns, one on the left and one on the right, but the vertical section in the center, between them, is a very important column unto itself. It not only demarcates the left and right columns, but it serves as a visual metaphor, with multiple meanings.

First, the central column of the CalmUp® Journey symbolizes the core of the human being, your center and your power, your essential self. In fact, the words "core" and "courage" come from the Latin root *cor*, meaning "heart"—and isn't that just about where we place our finger when someone instructs us to "point to who you are"?

Second, the central column represents the process of transformation. You might imagine the column in the shape of a spiral, to depict flexibility of movement, both upward and downward—and also nonlinearly: core change is hardly ever a straight shot skyward or, thankfully, a vertical drop!

You'll notice that there are no instructions for writing anything in the central column during your CalmUp® Journey, so it will be easy to forget its value in just being there, with no obvious practical function. Likewise, the core can be easily forgotten on your path, so, third, let the central column remind you of the importance of *being* in bliss rather than constantly *doing*. And while you're in that state of being, consider that you're being bliss itself! As George Fowler writes, "Life is not something that I *have*, but the Something that I *Am*… The place of our Source and fulfillment and bliss is only found within."[7]

If this concept of the core seems too philosophical, consider the backbone. You don't see your backbone, yet you use it all the time. Your backbone works hard for you 24/7, supporting you as you drive, walk, type, eat, laugh, cry, sleep. As you use the CalmUp® Journey, your growth and self-empowerment depend on honest self-reflection, which means returning to the core.

What other meanings does "core" elicit for you?

Becoming Light

The CalmUp® Journey is neither about being stuck in negativity nor about looking through rose-colored glasses. Our experiences, feelings, and actions are rarely black and white—there's usually a little gray in good or bad, right or wrong, okay or not okay—so it's vital to our humanity that we recognize the infinite possibilities and the necessity for the whole.

The whole allows for the darkness and the light. Our darkness, or shadow self, serves our path as constructively, as meaningfully, as does our light, or higher self—which is why the CalmUp® Journey invites your examination of both. Discerning when the shadow is operating allows you to identify and choose an opposite feeling state, one authentic to your core, thereby illuminating the darkness.

---

7   George Fowler, *Dance of a Fallen Monk: The Twists and Turns of a Spiritual Life* (Reading, MA: Addison-Wesley, 1995), 301–305.

Beginning at birth, we all have our own light to shine. My hope with the CalmUp®️ Journey is that we each rediscover and reclaim that light—and recognize that loving all parts of ourselves is important for the continuation of our human journey, individual and collective, on Earth.

Diving into the Darkness

To work with the whole, we must acknowledge that there is very real darkness in our world. Police officers, emergency-room staff, counselors, forensic specialists, military personnel, and the like spend a significant part of their lives face-to-face with the brutality of the human condition. We may be insulated from such tragedy; we may assure ourselves that those things happen to *other* people; we may deny that we, too, are capable of such darkness.

"How could she have done that to her children?" "What was he thinking?" Any act of violence clearly emerges from the dark, but what about the personal misdemeanors of judgment and gossip? If we can recognize the truth of our shadow in the small stuff, and fully see the world's darkest atrocities, we can acknowledge the possibility that, under the same circumstances, we might've done the same thing.

In Level II of the CalmUp®️ Journey, we acknowledge our darkness by noticing and listing the painful feelings related to our question. Only after immersing ourselves in, rather than denying, the genuine painfulness of the moment can we consider other realities. The following list may help you identify your feelings precisely.

Sample Painful Emotions:

angry, irritated, furious, fed up, pissed off, hurt, sad, disappointed, unappreciated, hopeless, helpless, worthless, grief-stricken, unloved, undeserving, jealous, scared, anxious, overwhelmed, stressed, turned off, uncomfortable, manipulated, victimized, pressured, over-accommodating, abandoned, lonely, broken-hearted, deprived, ashamed, needy, vulnerable, distracted, impatient, critical, criticized, distant, mournful, neglected, burdened, mistreated, hassled, rejected, inadequate, disconnected, resentful, isolated, withdrawn, rejected, defeated, dishonored, humiliated, superior, inferior, isolated, ignored, insensitive, shocked, reluctant, unstable, fragile, misunderstood

Your Turn:

In the left-hand box of the Level II row, list all the painful emotions you've experienced in relation to your question.

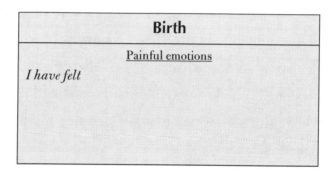

Birth

Painful emotions

I have felt

Leaping into the Light

In Level II of the CalmUp® Journey, in addition to acknowledging our darkness, we explore the possible expressions of our light by listing the feelings we *want* to feel. This doesn't mean that these feelings are "better," that where we want to be is "good" so where we currently are must be "bad." It's just a different choice, with a different outcome. Judgments like "good" and "bad" too easily become static labels, when, in fact, they can differ from person to person, from experience to experience, from moment to moment.

Who are we when we remove our mask? What are we like when we put aside our ego? Is there another reality than the one we've been feeling? Advances in mind-body medicine suggest so:

> Mood, attitude, and belief can affect virtually every chronic illness: fear, cynicism, as well as a sense of hopelessness and helplessness, can have a detrimental effect on health; whereas courage, good humor, a sense of control, and hopefulness can all be beneficial. Optimistic people are less likely to become ill and, when they do become ill, tend to live longer and suffer less.[8]

8   The Burton Goldberg Group, ed., *Alternative Medicine: The Definitive Guide* (Fife, WA: Future Medicine Publishing, 1993), 347.

It can be scary to go down a new or different path. We've been quite comfortable with our darkness—and we even developed an identity around it: our shadow self. At the same time, exploring a new path can be exciting and exhilarating. Consider your authentic self to be a new frontier! The following list can help you describe another reality of feelings, ones aligned with peace and joy.

Sample Peaceful Emotions:

amazing, ecstatic, excited, complete, strong, courageous, healthy, happy, relaxed, calm, peaceful, joyful, appreciated, appreciative, grateful, loving, loved, generous, hopeful, sincere, genuine, deserving, trusting, content, safe, fantastic, outstanding, creative, carefree, bright, clear-headed, liberated, committed, compassionate, empathetic, conscious, alert, awake, prepared, mindful, open, generous, flexible, cared for, caring, content, wonderful, beautiful, smart, positive, sincere, trustworthy, gentle, worthwhile, helpful, organized, sensual, turned on, connected, safe, understood, accepted, complete, fulfilled, authentic, confident, proficient, serene, justified, deserving, comfortable

Your Turn:

What peaceful emotions would you prefer to feel as your authentic self? You'll see, in the right-hand box of the Level II row, that we answer in the present tense, whether or not you're feeling those emotions now.

Birth
Peaceful emotions
As my authentic self, I feel

Follow Your Own Direction

Most people choose to leave the central column blank. The artist in you is welcome to color it, or even draw a spiral shape, as a reminder that you're working with the core at all times. You might consider that the core is actually working with *you*—as a pathway or channel through which the universal energy, or the Divine, ever-present, can flow when you're open and clear.

Key Points for Level II

✓ Acknowledge your darkness, your shadow self, by listing painful feelings related to your question. Then explore your light, your authentic self, by listing the peaceful emotions you would prefer to feel.

✓ The central column of the CalmUp® Journey has multiple meanings: (1) It symbolizes the core of the human being, your center and your power. (2) It represents the process of transformation. (3) It reminds you that you can *be* in bliss, rather than *do*, in this moment.

✓ Black-and-white thinking is discouraged in the CalmUp® Journey. You open to infinite possibilities and recognize the necessity for the whole.

✓ The whole allows for the darkness and the light.

CALMUP® Journey

Chapter 3

Level III:
Do Your Actions Show That You Want to Live?

That we are shaped by the culture we create makes it difficult to see that our culture is what must be transcended, which means we must rise above our notions and techniques of survival itself, if we are to survive. Thus the paradox that only as we lose our life do we find it.

Joseph Chilton Pearce
The Biology of Transcendence: A Blueprint of the Human Spirit

To Your Health!

*J*ust as we can't know the right side of the CalmUp® Journey without knowing the left, we can't know the top without knowing the bottom. Swami Rudrananda, or Rudi, taught that, in every situation, we have choices. One choice is to remain below the manifestation of energy that's taking place and consequently get "ground up." Rudi explained, "That is the acceptance of where you are against where you can be. Your choice is to rise above every situation."[9]

The farther we ascend the CalmUp® Journey, the more grounded we need to become. Any physical activity will get us into our body. Ideal activities are those that strengthen the core—for example, yoga, Pilates, and hula hooping. Does this mean you might want to do some sit-ups? Yes!

---

9   Faith Laxmi Stone, *Rudi and the Green Apple: A Story of Love and Transformation* (Rollinsville, CO: SGRY, 2000), 82.

In Level III, we consider our physical symptoms and the state of being that will create positive health. Along the CalmUp® Journey, after we explore our feelings, we examine what the body seems to be telling us. Typically, there is some action to take. Sometimes the most urgent action needed is to rest.

The Dark Side: Disturbing Physical Symptoms

Our body is always speaking to us, and when we truly listen, we can gain immeasurable insights about our state of being. Is your skin inflamed and (are you) angry? Are your muscles tight and (are you) anxious? Is your back aching and (are you) needing more support?

Identifying your various health conditions and disturbing symptoms won't likely be difficult, but if you draw a blank, the general terms below may help you describe specific symptoms.

Prompts for Physical Symptoms:

- Addictions
- Allergies
- Chronic pain
- Colds
- Diseases
- Gastrointestinal problems
- Gender-specific health issues
- Headaches
- Obesity and weight management
- Respiratory conditions
- Sexual dysfunctions
- Sexually transmitted diseases
- Sleep disorders
- Stress disorders
- Vision disorders

Such a list has proven helpful for clients using the CalmUp® Journey. For example, if you experience allergies, do you have a runny nose? Are you congested? Do your eyes feel itchy? If you experience a sleep disorder, do you have difficulty falling asleep? Is it hard for you to stay asleep? Do you experience hypersomnia?

How have you been feeling lately? Do you have any aches, pains, or sores? Inflammation or skin conditions? Have you been over- or under-sleeping? Are you suffering from a particular disease?

In the left-hand box of the Level III row, list all the disturbing physical symptoms you're currently experiencing, written in the past tense so that you can relegate them to the past!

Live
Disturbing physical symptoms
I have experienced

The Light Side: Positive Affirmations for Your Health

Louise Hay, one of the founders of the self-help movement, teaches that whatever you put your attention on in your life grows and becomes permanent. She pioneered the use of positive affirmations to create change in our life:

> *Learn to think in positive affirmations.* Affirmations are any statements you make. Too often we think in negative affirmations. Negative affirmations only create more of what you say you don't want... However, there is one point that is very important in this: *Always make your statements in PRESENT TENSE*, such as, "I am" or "I have." Your subconscious mind is such an obedient servant that if you declare in future tense, "I want," or "I will have," then that is where it will always stay—just out of your reach in the future![10]

Learning to think in positive affirmations and to write them down takes some practice. In Level III, we focus specifically on health affirmations. Note that your statement about your physical symptoms would be a negative affirmation if phrased in present tense.

---

10   Louise L. Hay, *You Can Heal Your Life* (Carson, CA: Hay House, 1984), 82.

The easiest way to write a positive health affirmation is to consider how you would rather be feeling physically or what you know your body needs, and write an "I am" statement like the samples below. You'll talk yourself into actually feeling and doing what you write! I'll get on my elliptical machine with no intention of doing so, and walk into work later with energy and great posture, the very thing I had written down for my positive health affirmation. Thus the seemingly magical shift from feelings into action.

To better understand the Level III process, see these sample pairings of disturbing physical symptoms and positive affirmations:

Sample Affirmations:

Live	Live
Disturbing physical symptoms	Positive affirmation for your health
*I have experienced **bloating, discomfort, tense jaw muscles, and swollen fingers from eating too much salt on my popcorn last night.***	*I am **prepared to start my day with a run to the park. I know that I'll feel so much better afterwards.***

Live	Live
Disturbing physical symptoms	Positive affirmation for your health
*I have experienced **a sore throat and a fever. My ears have been full, and my energy down.***	*I am **certain that the best thing I can do for myself today is to stay home from work and sleep.***

Live	Live
Disturbing physical symptoms	Positive affirmation for your health
*I have experienced **waking up with a killer headache. I've been congested and groggy.***	*I am **prepared to start my day by meditating.***

Live		Live
Disturbing physical symptoms		Positive affirmation for your health
*I have experienced **feeling physically drained and completely depleted.***		*I am **feeling stronger and healthier every day. My self-care is a priority today.***

Live		Live
Disturbing physical symptoms		Positive affirmation for your health
*I have experienced **nausea, stomach distress, diarrhea, and a sinking feeling.***		*I am **pain-free, safe, and secure. I trust that I am capable of managing everything that comes my way today.***

Also, "The List" in chapter 15 of Louise Hay's book *You Can Heal Your Life* offers a wealth of alternative thought patterns and affirmations for numerous physical problems.

Your Turn:

How would you rather be feeling today? What physical sensations would counterbalance your current pain with peacefulness? Notice, in the right-hand box of the Level III row, that we answer in the present tense—whether or not you're experiencing that state now—so that your future can become your present!

Live
Positive affirmation for your health
I am

Follow Your Own Direction

If you don't believe, in your gut, your positive affirmation for your health, you're wasting your time. If you write down somebody else's hopes and dreams for you, you're not following your own direction. Take a stand. What's important to *you*?

Key Points for Level III

- ✓ List your current physical symptoms and write a positive affirmation for your health.

- ✓ The farther you ascend the CalmUp® Journey, the more grounded you need to become.

- ✓ After you explore your feelings, examine what your body seems to be telling you. Sometimes the most urgent action you need to take is to rest.

- ✓ You write a positive affirmation because what you put your attention on grows stronger in your life.

CALMUP®Journey

Chapter 4

Level IV:

Will You Go Inward and Open Your Heart Today?

As I look back, my life has not been easy. However, throughout all these years, I learned about compassion, about caring for others. This mental attitude has brought me inner strength.

The Dalai Lama
An Open Heart: Practicing Compassion in Everyday Life

Open with Care

You've made it to the halfway point! Although every aspect of the CalmUp® Journey is purposeful, don't worry about making mistakes or taking a wrong turn. The CalmUp® Journey gently guides us to look inward. Now, in Level IV, we explore how to safely open the heart by transforming any fear or worry arising from your question into a constructive behavior. What heavy baggage can you leave behind? What do you choose to carry today?

The Dark Side: A Disheartening Image

When thinking about *anything*, we tend to come up with a corresponding mental image. And when that *anything* is less than positive, our image is usually a disheartening one. For instance, right now imagine being uncomfortably cold. Do you picture yourself in a snowstorm without a coat, shivering, with your arms crossed over your chest? Or do you picture yourself coming out of the shower, with no towel or bathrobe within reach?

You may ask why we focus on a disheartening image if, as noted in the last chapter, what we put our attention on grows.

Transforming fear and worry requires bringing them into full awareness. Fueled efficiently by fear and worry, the mind is a machine, automatically churning out corresponding images. We don't have to hang on to those images; we can see them and then let them go. And writing them down is a kind of safekeeping that, paradoxically, allows our attention to move on to something else.

Your Turn:

Think about your question. What do you fear or worry about in relation to it? What's your worst-case scenario? In the left-hand box of the Level IV row, describe the mental image you conjure up. See the sample responses on the next page.

Inward
<u>Disheartening image</u> *I have pictured myself*

The Light Side: A Self-Loving Visualization

Sadly, many of our habitual ways of thinking and being are self-destructive. As with any learned behavior, integrating a new, constructive way of being takes repetition by way of practice—without judging ourselves. Self-loving visualizations, like positive affirmations, create *who we want to be*—with respect to our physical and emotional well-being. Science has corroborated the health benefits of such techniques:

Imagery can be a key factor in dealing with either a simple tension headache or a life-threatening disease. It is a proven method for pain relief, for helping people tolerate medical procedures and treatments and reducing side effects, and for stimulating healing responses in the body. Imagery can assist in clarifying attitudes emotions, behaviors, and lifestyle patterns that may be involved in producing illness. It can also facilitate recovery, and be used to help people find meaning in their illnesses, cope more effectively with their health problems, and come to grips with life's limitations.[11]

When we release old patterns of darkness and consciously adopt patterns of light, we open to accepting and loving ourselves. And accepting and loving ourselves allows us to accept and love others more authentically.

To better understand the Level IV process, see these sample pairings of disheartening images and self-loving visualizations:

Sample Self-Loving Visualizations:

Inward	Inward
Disheartening image	Self-loving visualization
*I have pictured myself **running on a hamster wheel, getting nowhere fast.***	*Today I visualize myself **remaining mindful and sitting quietly in the backyard before dinner.***

Inward	Inward
Disheartening image	Self-loving visualization
*I have pictured myself **becoming irritated and losing my temper with my co-worker, being sent home, losing my job, and getting kicked out of my building—my day going from bad to worse.***	*Today I visualize myself **counting to 10 before I speak. I find something kind to say to my co-worker, and we complete our project together. My day keeps getting better and better.***

---

11 The Burton Goldberg Group, ed., "Guided Imagery," in *Alternative Medicine: The Definitive Guide* (Fife, WA: Future Medicine Publishing, 1993), 247-248.

Inward	Inward
Disheartening image	Self-loving visualization
*I have pictured myself **being sick in bed so that I could finally get some rest.***	*Today I visualize myself **taking time to rest for 20 minutes after work.***

Inward	Inward
Disheartening image	Self-loving visualization
*I have pictured myself **having a big fight with my partner over the money I spent.***	*Today I visualize myself **sitting down and creating a budget.***

Inward	Inward
Disheartening image	Self-loving visualization
*I have pictured myself **having another crappy day today, experiencing more car problems, having no time to eat lunch, wasting my time at work, and—the highlight—falling asleep watching television again.***	*Today I visualize myself **having one of the best days of my life. I make it into work with time to spare. I treat my boss to lunch. I write down all the ideas I've been thinking about. My evening is full of possibilities.***

Your Turn:

In the right-hand box of the Level IV row, imagine a self-loving visualization that softens your disheartening image. Trust that you have the power to turn a wish into reality.

Inward
Self-loving visualization
Today I visualize myself

Follow Your Own Direction

This is *your* CalmUp® Journey, so creativity is encouraged. What artistic mediums can you integrate? Can you create a collage, write a poem, play an instrument, dance, or pantomime to express your Level II emotions or Level IV disheartening images? When the mind is bypassed, fresh perspectives and possibilities can arise.

Key Points for Level IV

✓ You safely open your heart by transforming any fear or worry arising from your question into a constructive behavior.

✓ Look inward and conjure up a disheartening image followed by a self-loving visualization.

✓ Accepting and loving yourself allows you to accept and love others more authentically.

✓ Creativity is encouraged. What artistic mediums can you integrate?

CALMUP® Journey

Chapter 5

Level V:

What's Your Contribution to Society?

Agape has nothing to do with like-minded people supporting each other. Story after story tells of foreigners, aliens, and misfits being welcomed. The point is to create a world community that transcends religious allegiance and nationalism.

Thomas Moore
Writing in the Sand: Jesus and the Soul of the Gospels

Your New Frontier

*I*n Level V, the focus is no longer on the self alone. We're ready to consider the "other" in relationship and community. When we begin to experience inner peace and joy, we eagerly want to share it with others.

If you're finding inspiration along your CalmUp® Journey, an important consideration at Level V is the implication of that inspiration for the larger world. If you feel overwhelmed by this notion, then start small: define your sphere of influence, your community, as the people emotionally and/or geographically closest to you. If you're not overwhelmed in the least, then consider the world's hungry and homeless, its poor and war-ravaged, its beaten and enslaved.

Apathy, judgment, superiority—these are some of the ways we try to separate ourselves from others, perhaps defense mechanisms against taking on another's suffering in addition to our own. A separate or defensive state of being drains our energy, but rather than recognize that we choose our state of being, we blame others for how bad, lonely, bored we feel.

It's ironic that one of the roots of our suffering, per Eastern and Western spiritual traditions, is the illusion of our separateness. Pragmatically speaking, unless you're going to live off the land in solitary bliss, you can't separate yourself from the society you interact with daily in order to live your life. And living in community, as such, means being accountable for our choices, as their consequences rarely stop at self but ripple out to our family, our friends, our colleagues, our planet. Rather than continue to blame others and block our healing, we can create peace through introspection and gratitude. Consider this notion from an alternative method of Japanese psychotherapy:

> How often is our attention wasted on judging, criticizing, and correcting others while we neglect the examination and lessons of our own life? While we can never know the actual experience of another, we know our own experience intimately. While we can do little or nothing to control how others treat us, we can do much to control how we treat others. And while we are often powerless to impose our choices on others, we make choices about how we shall live, moment to moment, day to day. Examining one's own life is profoundly sensible, though not necessarily comfortable.[12]

In Level V, we identify the counterproductive choices of our past and declare a corrective act of service to self and community.

The Dark Side: Making Poor Choices

When the impact of a choice isn't immediately visible or you're not already aware of it, how will you know when you've made a poor choice?

You may learn of others' reactions—and not necessarily to what you did but to what you *didn't* do. A "sin of omission" is as harmful as a "sin of commission." Could something you avoided doing have had a negative effect on others?

---

12 Gregg Krech, *Naikan: Gratitude, Grace, and the Japanese Art of Self-Reflection* (Berkeley, CA: Stone Bridge Press, 2002), 13.

In the left-hand box of the Level V row, record the poor choices you've made related to your question and their impact on others. See the sample responses on the next page.

Society
<u>Poor choices impacting others</u>
My poor choices have included

If you think your choices have all been impeccable, look again. None of us is perfect; none of us acts ideally or authentically 24/7. And who knows that better than our friends, family members, and coworkers! Asking one of them for input should elicit something that rings true for you.

The Light Side: Being of Service

In today's challenging world, it's pretty easy to figure out where we can be of service. A simple thank-you note or a held door may be all it takes to launch someone into a better day. Other times, you may need to do or say something particular to make things right with another person. Can you "eat crow"? Can you be the one to make the first move? Having opened your heart in Level IV, you've opened to the opportunities for practice that will come your way in Level V.

Even though the Level V heading is "Society," you can be of service to yourself, even when the intended focus is "other." Putting yourself first can actually better serve others. Consider the new mother who chooses to take a nap when her infant is napping so that, rested, she can be present to those around her.

At first glance, some of the sample declarations of service below may seem to have nothing to do with being of service. However, by becoming increasingly aware of the quality of our health, the impact of our behavior, and how we direct the flow of our energy, we can open to healing, peace, and wholeness. And it's our wholeness, our integrity, that makes us better partners, friends, parents, children, employees, employers, citizens, and leaders.

Sample Declarations of Service:

Society	Society
Poor choices impacting others	Being of service
*My poor choices have included **overeating last night**, which has increased my risk for certain diseases and burdened the health-care system.*	*With integrity, I will **let go of junk food for one day a week.***

Society	Society
Poor choices impacting others	Being of service
*My poor choices have included **speaking meanly to my family** and not being respectful to them in general. I've modeled poor behavior for my children and not shown my partner how much I love him/her.*	*With integrity, I will **take a deep breath before I speak**. I know that by becoming aware of how I speak to my family, I will also speak carefully to others.*

Society	Society
Poor choices impacting others	Being of service
*My poor choices have included **losing my temper at work today by yelling at my coworker** in the middle of the meeting.*	*With integrity, I will **email an apology for my behavior** to everyone who attended the meeting. I'll also apologize directly to my coworker. I'll be more of a team player and not take things so personally.*

Society	Society
Poor choices impacting others	Being of service
*My poor choices have included **becoming overly focused on my own needs**, making more money, and looking good, all of which have impacted the quality of my relationships.*	*With integrity, I will **research volunteering opportunities** for even just one hour a week at the closest service organization in my county.*

In the right-hand box of the Level V row, record what you will say or do with integrity to be of service to yourself and your community.

Society
<u>Being of service</u>
With integrity, I will

Follow Your Own Direction:

It can be challenging to consider new choices based on integrity and accountability to the greater whole. Making new choices is an act of will. As you ascend your CalmUp® Journey, you'll become increasingly aware of your willpower.

Caroline Myss, an expert in the field of energy medicine and human consciousness, speaks to the importance of surrendering your personal will to divine will.[13] While I was writing this very point, my dogs bounded over, demanding a walk. What else could I do but surrender? My will wanted to finish this chapter, but it was a Sunday and I had plenty of time. Was the blue heron I saw on that walk a divine reward?

How can you surrender to a higher will today? What new, amazing direction can you take? Might your new choice bring a better day?

---

13 Carolyn Myss, *Anatomy of the Spirit: The Seven Stages of Power and Healing* (Boulder, CO: Sounds True, 1996), 2 audio cassettes.

✓ Your focus is no longer on the self alone. Evaluate how your poor choices are impacting others, and determine what you can say or do with integrity that will serve yourself and your community.

✓ What implication does your inspiration have for society and the larger world?

✓ When you become increasingly aware of the quality of your health, the impact of your behavior, and how you direct the flow of your energy, you can open to healing, peace, and wholeness.

✓ It's your wholeness, your integrity, that makes you a better servant in the world.

CALMUP® Journey

Chapter 6

Level VI:
Are You Connected to Spirit?

Spirituality is about being able to see what's wrong with ourselves, accepting the idea that we can change, and then showing a willingness to actually transform ourselves. Rather than relying on an ego that says, "I'm okay and the rest of the world is a problem," it's the capacity to say, "I'm willing to see that I need to improve myself, and I'm willing to give before I take.

Karen Berg
God Wears Lipstick: Kabbalah for Women

Rising to the Occasion

I used to think I knew what spirituality was about. I regularly meditated and did yoga; I learned to walk and eat mindfully; I even went to an ashram for a retreat. It took me almost forty years to discover I had only a glimpse. Sure, I learned to be still, to listen to my heart, to allow for the moment. However, there's a great deal more to learn when it comes to "being spiritual."

In discussing the spiritual component of the CalmUp® Journey, I've tried to be inclusive rather than exclusive. We each hold different beliefs about spirituality, which some of us express through a particular religious faith. God, Yahweh, Allah, Creator, Higher Power, Nature, Great Spirit, the Great Unknown—no matter which entity you revere, or whether you consider yourself spiritual, religious, agnostic, or atheist, you are ready for Level VI of the CalmUp® Journey.

While spirituality is best understood according to your individual beliefs, to your own heart's truth, Karen Berg offers a compelling universal definition: "Spirituality is about accepting that our whole reason for being is to share."[14] Understanding spirituality as sharing, as serving others, allows for commonality not only across religions, but also across cultures, nations, neighborhoods, families, and individuals. *Love thy neighbor as thyself.* And when we grapple with that, that's being spiritual, too!

In Level VI, we connect with our spiritual nature by replacing our illusions with creative openings. An opening may occur through personal prayer, truth-telling, exploring an opposite interpretation, letting go of expectations, practicing a virtue, or any meaningful personal experience.

The Dark Side: Clearing Your Mind of Illusions

You may be surprised at what will pour out of you in this clearing. Think of "clearing" as a form of venting. When you clear, you get it all out. What are your biggest worries about your question? Do you have any deep fears related to it? What are your most discouraging thoughts? The dark side isn't soft and gentle; expect harsh and ugly. You may opt to shred or delete your CalmUp® Journey later, so that your writing remains private.

Level VI provides a wider lens through which to view your question. During one of my own CalmUp® Journeys, for instance, I realized that I'd been attached to this illusion: "In order to complete something important (like this chapter), I need to be tense and anxious." This demeanor had given me the illusion of being in control. I thought that going around all tense and busy with deadlines motivated me to get my work done. Talk about crazy! Well, illusions *are* pretty crazy.

The wider lens illuminated a deeper behavioral pattern, and once I acknowledged it, I could open to a new, more constructive truth.

---

14   Karen Berg, *God Wears Lipstick: Kabbalah for Women* (Los Angeles: Kabbalah Publishing, 2005), 80.

Typically we think of an illusion as a distortion of reality. Yet, have you noticed that it can sometimes be challenging to determine what is real and what is your mind's story? Consider, then, that an illusion can simply be any negative belief or thought pattern that brings fear or pain.

Your Turn:

On the back side of the CalmUp® Journey, in the left column, clear your mind...or vent! Let the darkness that arises flow out. Just write and write and write. You can explore, journal, or list what's bothering you related to your question. When you're not sure how to start, you can expound the feelings you listed in Level II. For instance, "I feel mad because..." It may take you an entire page. Don't be alarmed if it takes three or more pages. See the sample response on page 45.

To maintain safety as you clear, allow the dark to come to the surface without screaming, hitting someone, breaking something, or engaging in any other abusive or addictive behavior. You'll find that darkness can arise in a nonviolent manner.

> Clear your mind by listing or journaling all
> your <u>worries, fears, and discouraging thoughts</u>
> about your question.

After you clear your mind, return to the front side and, in the left-hand box of the Level VI row, record in the past tense any illusions related to your issue. For instance, how might you summarize the negative thought patterns you've been telling yourself? Is there a primary belief causing you pain? See the sample responses on page 46.

Spirit
<u>Illusions</u>
(First clear your mind on the back of this page.)
I believed

The Light Side: Opening to Creative Transformation

Once you recognize your illusions, your mind is available for fresh, transformative ideas. A creative opening can occur any number of ways. I open to new truths through personal prayer upon awakening in the morning. Prayer is encouraged in Level VI, but if this opening isn't agreeable to you, consider opening to new truths by simply turning your illusion around. That's the joy of paradox: we can see something in a whole new light by exploring its opposite!

Letting go of expectations is yet another way to open. When you let go of expectations, you let go of any possible outcome—including positive ones. For instance, in my example on the dark side, I would motivate myself with the pressure of deadlines, then experience annoyance and fear when I was unable to meet them. On the light side, I was reminded that my intention is to support people to experience better days. Even though helping others is a positive way to motivate myself, isn't that still an expectation? When I let go of all expectations, I open to a better day right now.

You can experience an opening by practicing a virtue. Among the myriad virtues, consider forgiveness, gratitude, reverence, grace. Is courage important to you? How about tolerance? What virtues do you most uphold in yourself and admire in others?

A creative opening can happen through any meaningful personal experience, too. Seeing a baby, looking into a loved one's eyes, sharing kindness, returning to love, reading or writing poetry, smelling flowers, listening to birds sing, tasting snowflakes, dancing, making love, cuddling with your pet—who doesn't open just reading this list!

For my personal example, being tense and anxious gave me the illusion that I was in control. On the light side, I engaged in personal prayer and opened to being calm and fun-loving by going out with my family to a movie for a change of pace. My new truth was a reminder that God is in control, not me.

Spirit works in mysterious ways and not necessarily the way *you* think things should be. The paradox is that by becoming calm and fun-loving, taking better care of myself, and being easier to live with, I am able to complete this chapter with the love and support of my family—and my editor!

Sample Back Page:

Clear your mind by listing or journaling all your <u>worries, fears, and discouraging thoughts</u> about your question.	Allow your mind to become radiant by brainstorming <u>encouraging and hopeful ideas</u> about your question. What statements might a best friend, lover, or counselor offer?
I'm sick of _____. Nothing is ever going to change. I'm afraid that _____. There's nothing I can do to make things better. It's hopeless. It sucks that _____. If only _____. It's just not worth it. I'm wasting my time. If it's not one thing, it's another. They always _____. If he does that one more time, I'm going to _____. I can't stand how she _____. I should have _____. I'm never going to learn. Why can't I just shut my mouth?	*Every day is getting better. I can see small changes, and I know that I'm moving forward. I feel safe when I _____. I'm hopeful that _____. When I trust my judgment, I can accomplish just about anything. When I look for the good in people, I find it. I really like how she _____. I appreciate how he _____. I'm capable of setting limits for myself. I can also speak up for myself. I'm so glad that _____. Thank goodness that I _____.*

Sample Creative Openings:

Spirit	Spirit
Illusions (First clear your mind on the back of this page.) *I believed **that I don't have a chance to accomplish my goals. I've been foolish by setting my sights too high.***	**Creative openings** *I open to **taking a leap of faith while also making concrete plans to follow through with my mission. I prefer to feel courageous and move forward with co-creating this project. Not taking a chance would be foolish.***
Spirit	**Spirit**
Illusions (First clear your mind on the back of this page.) *I believed **that if my rating didn't go up to at least a 7, then I was doing something wrong or this tool would never work for me. Sometimes I've felt like I couldn't talk to my partner without fighting and criticizing.***	**Creative openings** *I open to **expressing love with my partner and being thankful for the love that we share. I feel honored to be accepted as I am. It's not my rating that's important; it's allowing me to accept being a 4 today. Perhaps I can do something to help make someone else's day a little better.***
Spirit	**Spirit**
Illusions (First clear your mind on the back of this page.) *I believed **I just can't make it through this chaos. I would've probably ended up getting really sick.***	**Creative openings** *I open to **a successful, productive experience. I pray that I can simultaneously support the project and take care of myself. I'm grateful for the number of people stepping up to help. Together we can create something special.***
Spirit	**Spirit**
Illusions (First clear your mind on the back of this page.) *I believed **I don't have it in me to be a good father. I really blew it. If only my own dad had been there for me when I was a kid, I might've known what to do.***	**Creative openings** *I open to **sitting in the sauna and letting all my fears melt away. I'm a pretty decent father. I may not be perfect, but I'm learning to be there more for my kids. I can be gentler with myself and with the kids. I think I can ask for forgiveness and let them know that I'm never going to give up.***

Spirit	Spirit
Illusions	Creative openings
(First clear your mind on the back of this page.) *I believed that I would always be overweight.*	*I open to spending a couple of hours doing yard work today. Spending time in the yard is my way of keeping active. I can burn calories and not eat while I'm working. I pray that I can love myself no matter what I look like. Thank you, God, for reminding me that people who care about me will look past my waistline.*

Your Turn:

In the right column of the back side of the CalmUp® Journey, brainstorm some fresh, optimistic ideas about your question. In fact, you can record here *anything* that comes to mind. See the sample response on page 45.

> Allow your mind to become radiant by brainstorming encouraging and hopeful ideas about your question. What statements might a best friend, lover, or counselor offer?

Return to the front side and consider closing your eyes and spending five to ten minutes in silent prayer. Perhaps you prefer to open by going outside for a run or taking a peaceful walk in nature. How do you encounter bliss? Afterward, in the right-hand box of the Level VI row, record in the present tense your desired creative openings. You may phrase it as a personal prayer, a new truth to internalize, or a virtue to practice. Whether or not you choose to spend time in silent prayer, most everyone can list reasons for being grateful. See the sample responses on page 46.

Spirit
<u>Creative openings</u>
I open to

Follow Your Own Direction

The CalmUp® Journey is a *flexible* guide. As you get more comfortable using it, you may choose to move through the columns and rows with your own sense of direction: left side to right side, top to bottom, odd then even rows, randomly. For instance, if you're feeling especially angry, you may want to clear your mind or consider a dark image first. The intention isn't to cut corners, but to tailor the guide so that it best supports your having a better day.

Key Points for Level VI

- ✓ Clear your mind by listing or journaling all your worries, fears, and discouraging thoughts about your question; then identify the primary illusions (fearful beliefs) you've held.

- ✓ You connect with your spiritual nature by replacing your illusions with creative openings.

- ✓ When you understand spirituality as sharing, as serving others, you can more easily *love thy neighbor as thyself*.

- ✓ The mystery of paradox is that sometimes you can see something in a whole new light by exploring its opposite.

CALMUP® Journey

Chapter 7

Level VII:
Will You Cross the Finish Line?

—————

Embrace this one solitary truth—you were born to become the-best-version-of-yourself—and it will change your life more than anything you have ever learned.

Matthew Kelly
The Rhythm of Life: Living Every Day with Passion and Purpose

Making the Choice

*Y*ou've made it to the top. The duration—how long it took you to complete your CalmUp® Journey—and the intensity—how easy or difficult your voyage was—are not important. What matters now is whether or not you're prepared to make a conscious choice for your day.

Take one deep healing breath and review where you've been on your CalmUp® Journey. Can you simply accept and love *all* parts of yourself? Remember that we need *all* parts of ourselves to create our wholeness.

Note the initial letter of the five headings: Birth, Live, Inward, Society, Spirit. This is a reminder that you are capable of being in BLISS today. David Deida gives us a view of our blissful nature:

> Just driving in your car, wanting nothing, watching the trees go by, can be an epiphany of perfection. Deep sleep, orgasm, a day of fishing, looking into an infant's eyes, these occasions can relax you from your search long enough to realize that

you already have what you seek, that what appearances promise is a revelation of your own deep and inherently blissful nature. You *are* that which you seek, but you have left your own deepness and are looking elsewhere… Your ultimate desire is for the union of consciousness with its own luminosity, wherein all appearance is recognized as your deep, blissful nature, and there is only One.[15]

You've ascended to the level of Spirit. Now, with complete awareness, you have the opportunity to cross the finish line by choosing how you wish to express yourself on this one, glorious day.

Dr. David R. Hawkins, a psychiatrist who has scientifically studied levels of consciousness, asserts, "The self-evident isn't arguable."[16] We have the ability to differentiate between high and low energy patterns. For instance, we prefer self-love to self-loathing, clarity to confusion, yes to no. You've learned to discern the dark and the light, to accept both sides and allow for loving *all* of yourself. Self-acceptance is crucial to Level VII of the CalmUp® Journey—and is something you'll sense energetically with more and more practice.

Remember your question? Identifying its answer is not the aim of Level VII. The answer will come in its own time; perhaps you've already received it. Sometimes the answer will come instantaneously, just by virtue of having asked the question. Other times, it will show up unexpectedly weeks or even months later. Either way, it's your choice to listen (or not) to the answers you receive. Can you accept living without an answer?

In Level VII, we make two conscious choices:

(1) How will I empower myself today?
(2) What will I do to share or serve today?

---

15 David Deida, *The Way of the Superior Man: A Spiritual Guide to Mastering the Challenges of Women, Work, and Sexual Desire* (Boulder, CO: Sounds True, 2004), 156–157.

16 David R. Hawkins, *Power vs. Force: The Hidden Determinants of Human Behavior* (Carlsbad, CA: Hay House, 2002), 133.

These choices are deeply personal. Only *you* know how to best empower yourself today; only *you* can decide what you'll do to share or serve today. These questions can help you access your most constructive conscious choices:

Questions to Support Decision Making for Choice #1:

- What does your authentic self ask of you today?

- What, if anything, have you been avoiding today?

- What, if anything, needs fixing today?

- What's one thing that, if you accomplish it (or at least begin it) today, you'll feel fulfilled?

- What will give you energy today when it's completed?

- How do you wish to express yourself today?

- What will bring you joy today?

Questions to Support Decision Making for Choice #2:

- What can you do to help someone else today?

- Who could use your quality time today?

- What can you do unconditionally for a friend/neighbor/stranger today?

- What can you do today to show your partner/child/parent how much you love them?

- How can you act today to show reverence/respect/love even while doing your everyday routine?

- What, if anything, could you donate today?

- Where could you volunteer today?

Review what you've written so far on your CalmUp® Journey, and take one deep healing breath to acknowledge what you've accomplished.

In the left-hand box of the Level VII row, write your two conscious choices for today: (1) how to empower yourself today, and (2) how to share or serve today. You may wish to record these two statements in your datebook or on a note card to carry with you as a gentle reminder during the day. See the sample response in Appendix A.

Rate Your Experience

Having completed your ascent, in the right-hand box of the Level VII row, now evaluate your progress. As with your baseline rating, you'll score on a 1-to-10 scale how much peace and joy you're experiencing in relation to your question. Your final rating will likely be a higher number than your baseline, but it could remain the same or even be lower. Honor whatever progress you've made; and if your rating declines, acknowledge the attention you've given to your question. Sometimes a question can be so painful that we avoid it as a way of coping. When we finally face the question with the CalmUp® Journey, the rating may sometimes decrease due to feelings of discomfort in facing the pain. These painful issues may require the support of a professional counselor.

The process of change and growth occurs not by reaching the top of the Daily Ascending Tool or by having a high final rating, but by staying fluid, moving back and forth regularly. As explained by Rabbi Irwin Kula, "The dream Jacob had later in the desert is not about ascending or transcending, leaving what is earthly behind: It's about going up and down the ladder, bringing earth to heaven and heaven to earth."[17]

---

17 Rabbi Irwin Kula, *Yearnings: Embracing the Sacred Messiness of Life* (New York: Hyperion, 2006), 230.

Deep healing breath; conscious choices	
FINISH → *(1) Today I choose to empower myself by*	
(2) I share/serve by	
	Peace & joy rating 1–10 (low to high)

Follow Your Own Direction

Although you may prefer the view from the top of the CalmUp® Journey, lingering there attached to the outcome can result in a hard fall to the bottom. How about getting curious and excited about waking up tomorrow to ascend again? If you anticipate a busy morning tomorrow, you may prefer to begin your CalmUp® Journey before bed. The critical thing is to make a plan for completing your CalmUp® Journey and stick with it. Integrating a new habit can take three to four weeks.

Key Points for Level VII

✓ Start with one deep healing breath. Can you simply love and accept all parts of yourself? Then consciously choose (1) how you will empower yourself and (2) how you will share or serve today.

✓ The initial letter of the five headings spells BLISS—a reminder that you are capable of being in bliss today.

✓ The answer to today's question will come in its own time. Can you accept living without an answer?

✓ The process of change and growth occurs not by reaching the top of the Daily Ascending Tool or by having a high final rating, but by staying fluid, moving back and forth regularly.

CALMUP® Journey

Afterword

You've crossed the finish line. You've made your choices for today. Could there be still more to this CalmUp® Journey? Working through the seven levels can enable us to let go of frustrating and fearful patterns in our life, but then what? How do we open to wholeness today?

The CalmUp® Journey was designed so that each level represents one of the seven colors of the visible spectrum. Remember learning as a child that white light comprises all the colors of the rainbow? That's wholeness. Imagine now a Level VIII, beyond the page, representing the color white—a harmonization of all the colors of the spectrum.

How might we ascend to that higher level and create global harmony, support the wholeness of life? Rather than ask your daily question for the sake of me and mine, can you expand its scope to consider the highest interests of all sentient beings? For example, instead of asking, "How can I continue to work for a company whose values I don't respect?" ask, "How can we all work our right livelihood?" You'll discover that the CalmUp® Journey easily adapts to "How can we..." questions.

How will you use your CalmUp® Journey to support wholeness? Will you work on self-change? Might you use the tool to promote self-healing? What about group change or group healing? Will you complete the CalmUp® Journey with your partner? With your coworkers or teammates? Can you integrate the CalmUp® Journey with professional treatment? Can you use it to support philanthropy? To create a comfortable living space? The possibilities are endless.

Each level of the CalmUp® Journey represents a different level of the human energy system, ordered by color per the visible spectrum. And each level of the CalmUp® Journey has a specific purpose just like each of our body's energy centers, or chakras, does. Scientific research into the CalmUp® Journey may support our understanding of health and disease. Here's a summary correspondence of the CalmUp® Journey levels and the chakras (integrated from works by Dr. Caroline Myss,[18] Dr. Anodea Judith,[19] and Dr. Rick Jarrow[20]):

Level	CalmUp® Journey	Color	Area	Energy
VIII	Ascending beyond the page	White	Beyond the crown	Soul
VII	Conscious choices	Violet	Crown area at the top of the head	Choice, co-creation, consequence
VI	Illusions and creative openings	Indigo	Forehead	Intuition, imagination, clear vision
V	Poor choices impacting others and being of service	Blue	Throat	Communication, creativity, will
IV	Disheartening image and self-loving visualization	Green	Heart	Giving, receiving, supporting others
III	Physical symptoms and positive affirmation	Yellow	Solar plexus	Self-esteem, ego
II	Painful and peaceful emotions	Orange	Sacrum, lower back, hips, and genitals	Feelings, sensations, emotions
I	Open-ended question	Red	Base of spine	Earth, connection with the life force

18   Caroline Myss, *Energy Anatomy: The Science of Personal Power, Spirituality, and Health* (Boulder, CO: Sounds True, 1996), 6 audio cassettes.

19   Anodea Judith, *The Chakra System: A Complete Course in Self-Diagnosis and Healing* (Boulder, CO: Sounds True, 2000), 6 audio cassettes.

20   Rick Jarrow, *Your Life's Work: The Ultimate Anti-Career Guide* (Boulder, CO: Sounds True, 1998), 6 audio cassettes.

Reaching the top of your CalmUp® Journey never means your ascent is over. It's more like a commencement, and you start anew every day. No one says it better than Caroline Myss:

> Your goal in your practice is not perfection. Your goal is to live consciously and in accordance with the highest degree of truth that your soul can maintain. You practice living with truth so that it becomes part of your soul.[21]

Are you ready for this daily journey to change, heal, and live fully?

---

21   Caroline Myss, *Entering the Castle: An Inner Path to God and Your Soul* (New York: Free Press, 2007), 29.

Appendix A

The CalmUp® Journey Sample Version

*T*he Sample Version on pages 61 and 62 is one of my personal CalmUp® Journeys. Until you become familiar with the CalmUp® Journey, refer to the Sample Version as you complete the Do-It-Yourself Version. You may also look back at the sample answers provided in the chapters.

CalmUp® Journey

Date: _____11-20-10_____

Instructions: Begin in the bottom row. Enter your responses, moving up from left to right.

FINISH → Take one deep healing breath. Can you simply accept and love *all* parts of yourself and make the following conscious choices for today? *(1) Today I choose to empower myself by choosing only one or two items on my to-do list.* *(2) I share/serve by spending quality family time.*	Having completed your ascent, rate the amount of peace and joy that you are now experiencing in relation to your question. *(10=highest peace & joy; 1=lowest peace & joy)* *10* Rating 1–10
Spirit	**Spirit**
What illusions have you held? To answer this question, first clear your mind on the back of this page. *I believed that I needed to make a big dent in my to-do list to feel peaceful.*	What are your desired creative openings? Phrase it in the present tense as a personal prayer, a new truth to internalize, or a virtue to be integrated. *I open to gratitude on this amazing morning of snuggling with my family and dogs in bed.*
Society	**Society**
What poor choices have you made related to your question, and how have they impacted others? *My poor choices have included getting a parking ticket downtown yesterday—a wasted expense.*	What will you say or do with integrity while being of service to yourself and your community? *With integrity, I will take care of my responsibility and pay the ticket tomorrow morning. Today is for me and my family.*
Inward	**Inward**
What disheartening image have you pictured related to your question? *I have pictured myself getting sick from overworking and needing to stay in bed.*	What self-loving visualization can you imagine? *Today I visualize myself taking my to-do list and dividing it up to complete throughout the week. I have a great day with my family and time for me.*
Live	**Live**
What disturbing physical symptoms have been draining your energy? (Answer in past tense.) *I have experienced fatigue, the very beginning of a headache, congestion, and a clenched jaw.*	As you prepare to take action today, consider a positive affirmation for your health. (Answer in present tense.) *I am ready to give myself a day of rest, recovery, and relaxation today.*
Birth	**Birth**
What painful emotions have you experienced in response to your question? (Answer in past tense.) *I have felt overwhelmed, afraid, incapable, nervous, vulnerable, and embarrassed.*	What peaceful emotions would you prefer to feel as your authentic self? (Answer in present tense.) *As my authentic self, I feel capable, confident, calm, trusting, loving, enthusiastic, and joyful.*
START → Write down one issue about which you have been experiencing heartache, distress, or curiosity today. Write your issue in the form of a question: *How can I…?* *How can I be in bliss today?*	Having initiated the CalmUp® Journey, rate the amount of peace and joy that you are experiencing in relation to your question. *(10=highest peace & joy; 1=lowest peace & joy)* *4* Rating 1–10

Can you conceive that your responses in the left column are not "bad" and those in the right column are not "good"? We need all parts of ourselves to create our wholeness.

Copyright © 2011 by Lorie S. Gose, Psy.D. All Rights Reserved.

www.drloriegose.com

Clear your mind by listing or journaling all your <u>worries, fears, and discouraging thoughts</u> about your question.

Overwhelmed by all the things I'd like to accomplish today:

- *update chapter 7*
- *write a second introduction for book 2*
- *write to attorney regarding form*
- *continue to explore key words for website*
- *scrub the bathtub so I can take a bath*
- *clean off my dresser*
- *put away my briefcase files*
- *pay parking ticket*
- *get a new calendar*
- *give the dogs a bath*
- *work out on elliptical machine*
- *grocery shopping*

Afraid that I won't accomplish certain things on time and then I'll pay the consequences.

Incapable of keeping a clean home.

Nervous and embarrassed about sharing my writing openly today for a sample CalmUp® Journey.

Vulnerable because it's hard not to wonder, "What will people think?"

Allow your mind to become radiant by <u>brainstorming encouraging and hopeful ideas</u> about your question. What statements might a best friend, lover, or counselor offer?

Taking a day of rest feels so healing and nurturing. I haven't written a CalmUp® Journey in a week, and it feels good to reconnect with myself.

I'm happy to share my writing with others if it will support them.

I can handle feeling a little embarrassed if this will help people have better days themselves.

I feel great about clearing my schedule today.

My home doesn't need to be spotless. It is what it is.

I'm so glad Dave just agreed to start our day sitting in the hot tub together. Forget scrubbing the bathtub!

Everything important on my list will get done in its own time. I don't have to do everything by myself either.

Taking care of me today is the best gift I can give myself and my family.

Copyright © 2011 by Lorie S. Gose, Psy.D. All Rights Reserved.
www.drloriegose.com

Appendix B

The CalmUp® Journey Do-It-Yourself Version

*T*he Do-It-Yourself Version of the CalmUp® Journey is on pages 65 and 66. Extra Do-It Yourself tools are provided in the companion book, *CalmUp® Journey Pages: Your Keepsafe for Better Days.* You can also create your own blank tool by drawing a core down the center of both sides of a piece of paper and then drawing six horizontal lines on the front to create seven sections of equal size.

CalmUp® Journey

Date: _____

Instructions: Begin in the bottom row. Enter your responses, moving up from left to right.

Deep healing breath; conscious choices **FINISH →** *(1) Today I choose to empower myself by* *(2) I share/serve by*	 _____ Peace & joy rating 1–10 (low to high)
Spirit	**Spirit**
Illusions (First clear your mind on the back of this page.) *I believed*	Creative openings *I open to*
Society	**Society**
Poor choices impacting others *My poor choices have included*	Being of service *With integrity, I will*
Inward	**Inward**
Disheartening image *I have pictured myself*	Self-loving visualization *Today I visualize myself*
Live	**Live**
Disturbing physical symptoms *I have experienced*	Positive affirmation for your health *I am*
Birth	**Birth**
Painful emotions *I have felt*	Peaceful emotions *As my authentic self, I feel*
One issue **START →** *How can I*	 _____ Peace & joy rating 1–10 (low to high)

*Can you conceive that your responses in the left column are not "bad" and those in the right column are not "good"? We need **all** parts of ourselves to create our wholeness.*

Copyright © 2011 by Lorie S. Gose, Psy.D. All Rights Reserved.
www.drloriegose.com

Back Page

Clear your mind by listing or journaling all your <u>worries, fears, and discouraging thoughts</u> about your question.

Allow your mind to become radiant by <u>brainstorming encouraging and hopeful ideas</u> about your question. What statements might a best friend, lover, or counselor offer?

Copyright © 2011 by Lorie S. Gose, Psy.D. All Rights Reserved.
www.drloriegose.com

Appendix C

The CalmUp® Journey Questionnaire

*T*he CalmUp® Journey Questionnaire is on the following page. After you complete it, cut along the dotted line at the margin. Fold the page in thirds, and you'll see that the address is printed on the back of the page, prepared for mailing (affix a first-class stamp in the upper-right corner).

Thank you for providing your comments about your experience with the CalmUp® Journey. Your feedback will be useful in supporting others to create better days.

1. How did you hear about the CalmUp® Journey?

    a. Friend
    b. Website (URL: _____)
    c. Advertisement/Literature (Source: _____)
    d. Other (Please specify: _____)

2. What were your base and final ratings for a recent CalmUp® Journey?

    Base: _____   Final: _____

3. Was your question for that CalmUp® Journey answered?

    Yes _____   No _____

4. How did you choose to empower yourself and share/serve for that CalmUp® Journey?

5. Rate your satisfaction with the CalmUp® Journey (circle one):

Extremely Very Satisfied Satisfied Neutral Dissatisfied Very Dissatisfied Extremely
Satisfied   Dissatisfied

6. In what way(s) has the CalmUp® Journey been useful for you?

7. What do you like the most about the CalmUp® Journey (if different from above)?

8. What do you like the least about the CalmUp® Journey?

9. What suggestion(s), if any, do you have to improve the CalmUp® Journey (the tool's appearance, the process, the manual, etc.)?

10. Do you give permission to include your comments, name or initials, and residence in future literature?

    Yes _____   No _____ / Name or Initials: _____

    City: _____   State: _____ / Email (for updates): _____

The address is printed on the back of the page for easy mailing. Thank you!

Dr. Lorie Gose
2000 Wadsworth Blvd., Unit #139
Lakewood, CO 80214
USA